STARSHINE ROAD

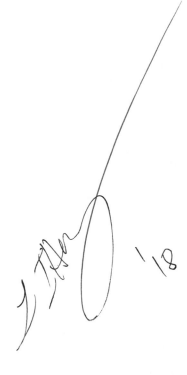

Starshine Road

L. I. Henley

perugia
PRESS

FLORENCE, MASSACHUSETTS
2017

Perugia Press extends deeply felt thanks to the many individuals who have contributed to the press over the years and whose generosity made the publication of *Starshine Road* possible. To make a tax-deductible donation, please contact us directly or visit our website. Perugia Press is a tax-exempt, nonprofit 501(c)(3) corporation.

Book design by Rebecca Olander, Jeff Potter, and L. I. Henley

Cover art is "Reclaimed Landscape: Flash Flood," mixed media, 49.5" x 36.5", by Barbara Spiller. Used with permission of the artist. Spiller's work can be viewed at barbaraspillerarts.com and joshuatreeartgallery.com.

Author photograph by Troy Miller. Miller's work can be viewed at imageryconcepts.com.

Library of Congress Cataloging-in-Publication Data

Names: Henley, L. I., 1984- author.
Title: Starshine Road / L. I. Henley.
Description: Florence, Massachusetts : Perugia Press, [2017]
Identifiers: LCCN 2017015237 | ISBN 9780997807615
Classification: LCC PS3608.E553 A6 2017 | DDC 811/.6--dc23
LC record available at https://lccn.loc.gov/2017015237

Perugia Press
PO Box 60364
Florence, MA 01062
editor@perugiapress.com
perugiapress.org
perugiapress.com

For Jonathan

CONTENTS

ONE

(I wore a black cape)

STORY

Little Child

     when you were being made
     your father became a wind tunnel

your mother scattered against the walls
the windows   with her cookbooks & tapes

Afterwards

he had to put her back together
one petal at a time

When it happened
conception made the sound of a shotgun

fired at close range   though they had expected
the reverb of a gong

Then

the toothed wheels of her parts
driven by a copper spring

Just think how you must have turned
as a waterwheel in space

SOMETIMES THREE HAWKS SITTING ON A FENCE POST MEANS WHAT YOU WANT IT TO MEAN IN VICTORVILLE, CALIFORNIA

Sometimes   during the usual months   it is spring in Victorville

You will not find the ordinary nest
with the ordinary eggs   all speckled & warm
but a half-eaten peach instead

As you would not touch a bird's egg   do not touch the bird's peach

*   *   *

Sometimes we need to be chosen
even though we are a sideways vine with a backwards bloom

My father
a cop
a white man

found his second mother

She was the granddaughter
of Black Elk   worked Citizen's Patrol
in Victorville   She called him   *my son*

He listened to her
the way young boys drink water
both hands around the cup   gulping

*   *   *

Seeds in the garden do what they want
Is it a bad seed because it didn't please us?
Try to find the sense that is not

You will happen across three hawks sitting on a fence post
& take it as a sign

But no   I'm telling you   those are black chickens

THIEVING-FEET

Shoeless in the November evening
crouched in the well of a pinyon
I watch my father who is in the middle of the backyard
between the chicken coop & garage
He's wearing gym shorts stained with axle grease & mustard

his black mustache
farmer's tan

praying or singing I can't tell which
but I have wished myself invisible

(Just two days ago
I woke him up in the middle of the night
he mistook me for a crook
he put his hand around my throat
until his eyes could focus & my thieving-feet shook)

He prays he sings he steps over a pile of leaves
finally he sees me   or someone like me

You forgot he says
to rake these

THE WORST

Four years old   my father's only child
he is teaching me how to shoot

Coffee cans perched on a fence in the desert
wingless rusted birds

The one in the middle
that one is a killer

The coffee can becomes
a man with many faces

who will follow me to the door
of my first apartment

then he'll be the old clerk
selling Lucky Strikes & Soju

then the guy from high school
who I'll marry & divorce

he'll be the lump in my breast

a branch in the street

the failed brakes in my car

he'll be a long walk down a bright hall
that narrows to an inch

But right now I am small
the pistol is small &

the pistol will jerk
How can my father know my heart?

I am distracted by something shiny in the dirt

for a moment I forget the worst
My first crystal   the size of a tooth

Steady   my father says   *Now shoot*

BUYING FOOD

I wore a black cape & yellow skates
he wore a Kevlar vest

We did not know we were afraid
Occasionally my ear would pop

against my father's gun-hip
bloom a silent red

When I hugged him
his gold star pressed cold against my cheek

He would see a pervert
squeeze my shoulder   point like a hunting dog

at a man buying birthday candles
or lingering by the cheese

Twenty years on the same streets
& *you just know*

No one seemed to notice how our blue shadows
swept the aisles

& so we lived without her   chose cans & boxes
that looked the most like food

Junk Pile as Seen from My Kitchen Table

From here
it is two inches of rust-red corral

a foot of chain-link
wooden posts every three inches

      a hanging gate

I am too far away
maybe thirty feet
eucalyptus leaves are blotting out the scene with their circles

It is a problem of perspective

The only thing clear is the stack of bricks
that are not the color of bricks
but loaves of bread

sourdough   rye   honey wheat

They collectively lean left
toward the chinaberry tree
& beyond that   chicken-wire housing a garden
of window glass

Beyond that

the shed with no doors
the neighbors spanking each other
the network of spitting roads
the highway where cars are going to Vegas   Salt Lake   Taos
At this rate
they'll never make it

I could watch you lean toward your desires all day
Please
promise me you are something close to content
at ease   something close
so we can keep on this way

DOG & HIS MAN

I find him or
he finds me in a box of dogs
We cry cold we live
in his shirt

two jackets

He cries for someone not dead
his wife he says her name
but I forget

You too big You too old
cry like that

He says *sit* & I don't
I say sit & he don't

*   *   *

My man he has no people
he hugs the ground he shakes the hands
of pear-colored leaves

I lead him I lead him
together we are a mirror
he looks more & more like me

What is a bad life? What is a good one?

My master   my man   he keeps us in shade
his hands grow thick as a tub
for me to drink from

Some people never see the winter sky he says

& it's true we can't come in
we can't get free of night
but we are never starless

*   *   *

Times we swim in the summer
we jump a locked gate

He lifts me he shakes *You too big!*

In the pool he speaks of tuna fish

Tuna the size of my leg!
Size of you!

He splashes my face

Salamander grow a new skin
ever three days

He's happy in the pool
in summer in the pool

sinks to the bottom
a lifetime   then pops up again

Electric blue!

*   *   *

You would eat me for my salt he say
You would eat me for my salt I say

The man is old   he shivers he dies slow
times we walk
we walk in snow   he shivers he dies slow

Somewhere up above it
just off the ground he say

He chatters he cries he dies slow

I pull out my bones & make a bed frame

I pull out my muscles
& make cushions

I lie on top of him
as a blanket

ECHOLALIA

At the county fair in Ferndale, California
the boys kill men on a 52-inch television
that shines from the bed of a black Hummer H3T

Hello boys what are you doing?   All at once: *Call of Duty!*

The recruiter says
They are learning & having fun

Look at the blood it looks so real

When have you ever seen blood spurt?
Call of Duty!

(What color is the lily?
What color is the lily?
Say red
Say red)

I want to understand the echo by stepping inside of its canyon
The dry grass would be unmoved
by the boom of a grenade on the base   but I would be ringing
I would be a jelly of bells

Hello down there
Hello down there
down there
down there

The color of the desert lilies might have been red
but the police weren't looking for them

They were looking for a body   a boy's
He was lured to Goat Mountain by a classmate
If you stand here at my bedroom window
you can see where it happened

This was long ago
but still you can hear its echo
each wave flailing through the walls like mutant bats

A monument crumbles   a leader   & no echo
A flower catches a boy's blood & catches a boy's blood
for decades

WE WERE AFRAID

& somewhere a ladder clanged
a boy went falling
a picture frame
an elephant carved out of Ivory soap

We were afraid

the phone rang
& a headless voice went breathing
a man into your ear

the fence rattled
an alley darkened

What did it mean that we were afraid
of small things
marble-sized explosions on a screen   blurs on x-rays
blurs in corners

everything
that never happened

(the wind pulled something succulent

from between its teeth)

TWO

(milk teeth)

SHOE TREE (A POEM IN TWELVE PARTS)

Where'd this town go? Ah. You can almost hear some singing.
—Elderly woman at Amboy gas station

preface

The tree in Amboy, California
creates itself
at the edge of a dry wash

Some say *tamarisk*
others say *old saltcedar*

To say *palo verde*
would show how little you know
about trees

To the east
a cinder cone
a lava field

To the west
a diner
a famous sign
a row of empty cabins
broken windows

There are shoes along
the highway
they are coming closer
  their tongues
   & laces
    trailing behind

We don't know
does the tree want them?

Does it call out?

1

It is tempting
to want
a *Book of Trees*
so as to try & find you in it.

How would you be listed?
What category?

Under *deciduous*—meaning,
"falling off at maturity"—
your shoe-leaves would
rust, age,
thud to the dirt.
The lighter ones, the child ones,
would be carried off
in the first gust.

Under *evergreen,*
your shoes would stay on, practicing their sway,
remembering winter
as a stitch to swallow,
a tolerable drop of poison.

If under *coniferous,*
we would come undone,
shaking & shaking your shoe-cones,
prying dagger-scales
in search of a seed.

2

Maybe, at first, we don't think
lumber—as in, "logs sawed for use"—
don't think *supply, fuel,*
pulp.

What other tree could postpone
our carpentry?

Death is the concern that comes before
provisions.

So. Never mind.

It's true, we judge a thing by
what it gives.

& so it must be we don't want what you have.
Your lumber is a load, a burden, a pile of things.
We see how it weighs on your shoulders.
Your walk
is a heavy one.

You make us wonder
about our debris,
our feet,
where we're going.

Tamarisk, forgive us.

See, even now
we want something.

3

The travelers,
they stand as close as they can get
while still outside your reach.

They'll stand in the middle of the road,
shading their eyes,
leaning back
to take in the whole of you.

*It's grown! It's shrunk! It's leaning
heavy on the left.*

They want to know what's changed.

Someone should stay & wait

& wait for a lateral bud to break
to see the unfurling
of white laces,
the emergence of leather & sole,
the first flash of eyelets
under sun.

A boy, maybe, of about twelve.
Someone with time, good eyes,
strange tools that fold
(telescope, camp chair, notebook)
& an appetite for *proving*.

4

The granny knot is to blame
for fallen shoes.
Of course, no one sets out to make
a failed knot, they think they've got
the usual *reef,*
saying to themselves the school-yard chant
right over left, then left over right.

We want our shoes to stay
where we've flung them, we want them
to sing from the highest branch,
want them to suspend like birds
with leather chests
riding a boundless current.

Shoe tree, what do you feel

when the knots begin
to loosen?

What do you feel about *us*—our skills, mistakes,
strength?

Judge by how hard
we throw.

5

How did this town begin & end
& leave so little in between?

A train came from a red horizon,
tracks fell into place
at the last possible second,
people were on it or just boxes, sacks of meal,
too hard to tell
until it passed.
It left behind a wooden station.

But that's not a beginning, not an arrival,
no person stayed.
& yet, there is a sign
pointing to a diner, & next door a row
of cabins, small & white
as milk teeth.

& that school, its rusted gate,
you can almost hear some singing.

6

Tree of Burden, Tree of Feet,
a confession:
I had a dream
after my divorce
that I was swinging around you
on a black rope of braided satin
tied to nothing I could see—swinging & swinging
& sort of flying,
surrounded by darkness.

Each time around you
I thought *power, power*
& each time gained a little.

It felt good between my thighs, the rope,
so I squeezed as I flew.

Power, power. It never stopped making sense
as most words seem to do.

So. Now. Awake, twisted in sheets,
I want to know,
where does this leave us?

7

Now there is the problem
of what to do with you.
Some say a museum,
others want you for
their private collection,
something to put above the mantel,
or perhaps in the middle
of a shopping mall. You could become
a new kind of wishing well—
a piece of modern art
something for people to interpret
or yawn at
or say they understand.

Soon,
as with all precious things,
we will shorten your name
& never think about the consequence.
Shoe Tree. Shoetree. As in, a device for keeping
shoes looking new & in shape—
the very antithesis
of what you are.

8

Once, a grieving mother was on her way to Arizona
& stopped to clean you up,
knowing a mess when she saw one.
Some boys were here, she thought. Some boys
have come & gone, the way they do,
& left a mess,
the way they do. So she spent the afternoon
climbing your branches, untying laces,
combing your needles.
She thought that cleaning & breathing in
the smell of feet would make her happy.
Every sneaker she untied
she cradled like a baby,
told it she was sorry & *hush, hush.*
In all, she took fourteen, the age of her son,
& for awhile she felt lighter
& you felt lighter,
but shoe by shoe
the heaviness was thrown back.

9

Some people leave one shoe & go limping,
while
others leave both
& resolve themselves to a new life
of parasites & fire walking.

It can be difficult to make a choice.
So most will keep
their shoes, which is still a choice.
& if a person doesn't stop their car at all,
this is a choice.
& if they don't come here, to Amboy,
this is a choice.
& if they never leave their homes again,
this is a choice,
even when all this is gone
& we have knocked ourselves unconscious.

10

Trees give us chocolate, coffee,
cloves, pecans. We know this as the truth:

we can build a house using a tree
& inside the house
eat the tree,
sleep on the tree, pull the tree
over us for warmth.

But you, with all of your gaping, flapping shoes,
what can you offer besides stories?

When we see your collection,
sometimes we joke out loud, *Ha, where's all the bodies?*
Then, when alone, *Where are the bodies?*

Many of us worry you are here for a reason.

We've come in a group
& we want to know.

11

Tamarisk, what or whom do you embody?
If a priestess, then this hard bench
makes sense, & I will draw back an imaginary curtain
to tell you my sins.

I have cursed ten million times, stolen matches,
wished for certain people to die,
made love through five layers of clothing.

If Death, then this umbilical cord makes sense,
& I will follow it back to you
when the scent of shoes overwhelms me. Let me be eighty
& slicing red onions with a good knife,
heating oil in a heavy-bottom pan, my old man
having just come in with wood from the pile,
& he is taking off his boots by the door,
the aroma overwhelming the onions,
& I will slip out quietly, following the chord.

If the Devil, then the desire to watch you from
between parted fingers makes sense,
& I love you just the same.

We, as a country, have done so many bad things.

Tamarisk, I'm not saying we deserve forgiveness,
but if we did,
would you give it?

THREE

(the blood & the water)

WE GIRLS

follow our mothers from room to room
of whatever house our fathers have bought or built or

not yet stepped foot into
or drunkenly wandered past

the way it has always been

we follow our mothers into their gardens
where they would like to read Lauren Bacall's biography
& be alone

the way it has always been

they undress for a bath
& we are there   asking *why*   *how*

staring like teenage boys at their tanned or pale flanks
gawking as they shave their legs

at the razor's smiling glint   how something so sharp
can be run along the skin   at the blood that seeps from nicks

mixes with water   the blood & the water
one carrying the other

the way it has always been

PARTIES

1

In a coat closet full of the half-naked sudden friends
the younger   older   painted faces

was it a boy   or was it a girl
with the short hair
the clown's face
who kissed my clavicle

as though lips could play the piano?

2

Never in our house   but this time   a party

& I remember only the waiting
sitting on the roof of my mother's powder blue Buick
the dent I left in the roof

Strange children will love the waiting far more than the getting
& take joy in the hours that pass   waiting
for hair to grow back   for a scab to form   for a house to fill
with enough friends for a party

Wish   star-fall   headlights   wish

It takes hours to fill a house this way
one at a time petals
dropped
in an earthen well

3

An invitation: *Will you come?*

Father planted big pine trees to keep
people on the street from seeing in   What he doesn't know:
the out is a bending back of the in

With his welder he works close to the sparks
he sparks he sparks he creates
a jailhouse for me to play in I rattle the bars

4

My mother & father are getting ready for a weekend of Halloween
parties   three parties two nights

They spent months collecting:

rabbit furs deer pelts bear claws shark
teeth rabbit feet snake skin &
wooden beads the size of my toes

He carved two spears
hammered leather pieces of metal
          spears
          to split open the dirt & suck up
the earth's mantel like
fruit punch in a straw if the right words
are said

From the doorway of their bedroom
I watch the laying on of leather & furs the darkening
of eyes with charcoal powders

the pulling on of leopard-print tights the bestowing
of bone necklaces
the adorning of wrists & ankles the tying on of masks

They laugh & they laugh
I am the only human left
to hear

the whoop of hyenas   the purr & chuff of Bengal tigers

the pleading of wolves   the rubbing together of cheeks & necks

No one at the parties will know
what they are

(deer-people? night-walkers? ghost-tigers?)

A cop & a housewife
eaten up?

THE ROAD A SILVER LADLE

My mother & I in the Buick
trying to get to her new apartment
when the clouds swarmed

she was trying to explain
separated

even after the car in front of us stalled
& the water rose   swallowed the tires

Now we could drown for all time
separated together from everybody for all time

      & her hands stayed so loose on the wheel

A drought   she thought   a walk across the Mojave
& then

water like thick honey from the comb

I'll know when it's time she said
to go out the window

HOME INVASION (LANDERS, CA 1992)

Mother had her pistol
I had bare feet   a child's gown

We hid behind our only tree

Winter was a pair
of silent mouths

we held closely

Junk Pile as Seen from inside the Junk Pile

Heavy blue insulators stolen
from New Mexico telephone poles
stove pipe pilfered from
a gutted cabin
stack of shingles the color
of lunch meat
plastic bin of horseshoes
cracking under sun
blades of a metal windmill mimicking
a clock face
ice cream scoop (existing) without
moving parts to break
There is nothing here
that I want
so then how do I
explain my love?

Cops

1

> I go to cop barbeques
> I go to their backyards & their homes
> I play with their daughters

Mrs. Lee
she's my keeper now

Every morning at 4 A.M.
my father drops me off
I crawl into Cindy's bed
& listen to her snore until sunrise

Mrs. Lee pours whole milk onto my Lucky Charms
slabs Betty Crocker onto my
Wonder Bread   says *eat it all up*

2

Yes Mommy & Yes Daddy & Yes Mommy &
YesDaddy&YesMommy

If one of them says just *yes* then
Officer Lee or Mother Lee snaps *YES WHAT?*

& the girl responds correctly

This morning Officer Lee threw
the oldest (Jessica) chest-first against
the wall because she didn't wash her cereal bowl

She's thirteen & her breasts are new
she hadn't gotten a chance to try them out before
they hit that wall

I always wash my bowl

3

In two months Officer Lee will smack
Jessica a few times for asking to date Cal
(captain of the basketball team straight-A student)

because Cal is black & captain of the basketball team
straight-A student black & those other things too
but he is black first

In five years Jessica will join the army cut
off her long blonde hair completely she'll eat all
of her food even if she only has
five minutes   she'll clean her bowl until it
almost sparkles
she'll use her toothbrush & her spit if she has to
she'll get the job done

4

Someday when Jessica is back in town for a visit she will
stand in line behind Cal at Walmart or Walgreens some place
like that she'll recognize him right away without even seeing
his face she'll think about their one kiss behind
the bleachers during halftime She'll remember the flexing

of his calves as his body rose toward heaven & the arc
of the ball before he won the game She'll remember each of the times
her daddy hit her Cal's smooth lips her father's uniform
the color of puke the roar of the stadium Mommy's fingernails
in her shoulder Cal's handwriting Daddy's lumbering shadow
his flashing metal star

STARSHINE ROAD

Remember the years out here when you thought you were dying
& weren't even close to an end   just walking with your books
to the bus stop

past that windowless shack where at 5 A.M.

the meth-heads had finally drifted off on Ambien?

Remember all the guys
who drove this washboard road
not always with the goal
of fucking you

the swirling dust lit
by a pickup's low beams

& some of them were actually worried

sixteen   alone in the desert
thirty minutes from town

& some of them remembered

about your neighbors

the ones who fired their shotguns at the sky
raked the dirt at 3 A.M.?

Remember the man with the handlebar mustache
pushing a black vintage baby carriage past your house
twenty times a day

the cats birthing in tool sheds   coyotes
the windowless shack?

Remember how you thought it would be—your death
in the cloaked roots of juniper
your hands bound with a purple sash

a lean coyote stepping overhead

that smell of buried treasure   finally?

HOUND

I did not want you when I first saw you
which is a response that you know
like your name & the names
you must be called
of which I too have called you
on all the nights that came before
You see   we people are like baskets
& sometimes like olives

there is a desire to always be filled

All that to say
we are afraid
& the filling is often a meatless
kind of shadow   You must be tired
Here is your bed & your bowl

How you knew I'd be out walking
you whose volume shifts like pop bottles catching rain
you with ribs like scratches
from a hand file
you hound with eyes too much like a man's

& how I thought
I could make it home without you trailing
behind   all of this serves as reminder
a string around the finger

I am not a closed book
not a pretty thing in a tower
there is meat in my coat pocket

THE BURDEN

I used to see how close I could get to a thing
without touching

Such as the man who worked at the health food store
when I was just graduating high school

He rode his bike to work   didn't have a car
said his muscles were from supplements & yoga

& I liked his shaggy auburn hair   blue eyes
his vocabulary of vitamins   the sounds of amino acids
Lysine   Glutamine   Carnatine   Taurine   the names
of precious stones

*   *   *

I admit to thinking hard on his cock
but not as much as the white hills of his ass
but not as much as his age   that twelve-year gap was the cake
on my tongue

He didn't have a bed so he invited me to a party in Gamma Gulch
(far from town far from cops)   It was everything he said
it would be   crystal gardens & teepees
couples sneaking away like quarter notes erased from the page

There were peacocks roving over the boulders   the males iridescent
          as oil spills   the females drab as nursing home drapes

I was dressed like a little present   a gold watch face   a collectible
Matchbox car   freshly minted cash   but I couldn't do it
the way I couldn't get my ears pierced when I was seven

both times thinking about the pain   the permanence

Our faces under the full moon said
we were disappointed

said we were destined
to make many mistakes

THERE IS SO MUCH TO SAY ABOUT LIGHTNING

for example

it precedes earthquakes or follows them
by seconds or years

it makes a tiger leave its cage
it is the reason for misplaced keys &
it sounds like salt rubbing against salt
in a glass on the shelf

Because each strike brings a new truth
we have not slept for years

& still we want to know
where will the next species
look to find us?

Not the ocean   not the sky
in those places
there is no sign that we have lived there
only the signs of accident   or sloth

NEW YEAR'S EVE AT THE HOTEL CONGRESS

Best thing about this place   you can come here on crutches
two days after knee surgery
your gut a prison cell full of lock-picking thieves

You can come here without your man   without your medication
without your own tarnished voice   & nobody will care

You can say to your friends
who are newlyweds

I would never hurt you & you don't need to know this but (lots of whisky &
       rum tonight huh?) the thing is that you two kiss so well
it makes me want to bow down & kiss your boot tips

so well that you deserve the world if the world is what you want   just think
you could be my first apology of the New Year

*   *   *

It's a miracle that I'm even here—
television prevents me from going out most nights

chains me to my bed most nights

feeds me puréed cauliflower night
after night

until the only words I love are *primetime*
& *cauliflower*   Call   a   flower
it's beautiful like *cancer*   (the word I mean
when you draw out the vowels)

In the lobby I passed a photo of Dillinger
the robber   & you know I think that if we'd been alive
at the same time we'd have been lovers

He's got a mustache   which I hate
but his eyes are black & reflect ghosts (which I love) &
even in the old black & white photo
I can see how they would have watched me

*   *   *

4 A.M. in many places   but this is the only place we can be sure of
What I said earlier   it was a very quick thought a jackrabbit
a whiskey slid across the wet bar kind of thought

& now it is blurrier than my face in the rusty mirror in the hall
that leads to my hotel room

more cold than
for example
the moments lying awake
next to a man
I don't like anymore
having just lied about needing him more than water

more confusing than
the knife in my own hand
up to my own throat
& the laughter gushing out

*   *   *

At the Hotel Congress in Tucson

you can see bullet holes in the wall
where the cops shot Dillinger & missed

You can smoke a cigarette & order
a vegan breakfast

even at 4 A.M.

THEY DANCED ME ALL AFTERNOON

It was my 24th birthday
& I wanted a divorce

My friends gave me a party
fed me olives   caramels
drank port

I was drowsy as a mop

One friend turned on music
then with cake-licked fingers
held up the corners of my mouth
& smiled me   while another friend held my waist
using one strong & tattooed arm

Someone moved my feet   pointed my toes
bent my knees

They danced me until I was
beating like a freshly made heart

        they blew my lost wishes
through the hair on my head
blew until the candles flickered
flickered & relit

FOUR

(bang   bang   bang)

DRIVING EAST PAST THE WIND FARM ON INTERSTATE 10 AFTER A YEAR OF UNEMPLOYMENT

White spinning turbines

they grow for miles   spilled
from a packet of seed

I am moving back
to the family cabin in Joshua Tree

sold my television
most of my furniture

Men climb up the sides
of the turbines   wind farmers

Everyone farms *something*

children
pain
gadgets

Not too far from here
rainwater makes
a mineshaft its vessel
& that's what worries me

I refuse to drown for a trove

WINTER'S HILL OR SUMMER'S LAWN

Grandfather & I   we made guns
out of anything we could find
shot cypress   hedges   cedar fences

Flying me in the two-seater plane he built
himself he would take his hands off the controls
& put them behind his head
to give me a little lick of death

In the home now—Winter's Hill
or is it Summer's Lawn?
some name with a season & a land mass—
my grandfather wears his flight jacket
over a uniform of navy-blue pajamas

The nurse pricks his finger
he winces   sucks in air

says he wants to watch the other people eat cake
We watch them eat it

In the courtyard:

What's holding all this up? he asks about the sky

A small plane overhead
coming into one of Redlands' private hangers
& he cups both ears with his hands to listen

I think I might have flown that plane

No I say as I always say *It was a P-47*

My grandfather makes his hands look like guns
points them at the sky

What kind of friend is the brain?

Pow pow pow he whispers
& then just as quietly
bang   bang   bang

A DOLLAR (FOR A FUNERAL)

The woman was still in love
I could tell by the way
her arms cradled

something swathed
Her glass eye was the color
of my coffee

it reflected the parking lot
arches   patrons with crew cuts
school books on loan
a shadow tied to a string

A dollar she said to me *a car wash*

It was a spell   it was a song
her rising open palms
My son she said *his funeral*

*   *   *

The woman was an immigrant
I could tell because
her syllables were like cherries
plucked by greedy birds
her sentence
an empty tree

A dollar? she asked
A funeral?

How to explain currency   ceremony

I touched her arm instead
but she dragged her cardboard sign
to the highway   like a slab
held it against the wind

My son it read *My son*

*   *   *

The woman was pregnant
Her feet spread like pancake batter
through rubber shoes

I'd seen her before   bathed in bubbles
fumes   hubcaps   washing cars
pumping gas   separating white light
into a spectrum of colors

She wanted to know the time
I looked up from my milkshake
parcels   watches   a dollar
fell from my sleeve   a green feather

She bent to it   her stomach growled

What could I say?

So young & yet the cracks on her hands
like bars on a tiger's cage

*   *   *

I'd seen her underneath a bench
hugging a dog for warmth

I'd given her a dollar then

& she asked again

to bury her son

She lived with him once
years ago   They washed the dog
in the bathtub every Saturday

Sundays they filled the dead father's
work truck with black cherries
pushed it into a canyon

made sunset for West Covina

The truck always came home
until   of course   it didn't

*   *   *

The woman had just died & come back

I knew because
people leaned toward her
then away

Each of us learned one new thing
but most forgot
instantly

What I heard   a melody
played on white keys

Son, son, fun-er-al, play a-long
with me!

I forget the rest

No one could drink
their coffee in peace
She was slick with afterbirth
her eyes were grey
& suspicious as newborn wolves

A dollar to make her go away   a hundred
Our arms to bite   our throats

*   *   *

The woman was a liar
I knew because I didn't believe her

Do you have a dollar for my son's funeral?

I asked her what happened

A boating accident   last week

Her husband & brother
her cousin & nephew & neighbors
all washing cars behind McDonald's

for her son   his funeral
I said I was sorry

The plane she said
it went straight down
how is it I'm alive?

& the fire   all the lint from the dryer
why hadn't I cleaned it out?

The heart defect   silent in the night

How could I have known? Tell me
how could I have known?

*   *   *

The woman had a mouth full of tiny shoes
When she hummed
I could hear a boy
awake too early
looking for his plastic car

Her breasts were blown glass
still molten
No one would touch her

not even her husband
who was behind Kmart
washing the trucks
of teenage boys

His tattooed hand opened to the dollars
opened to the quarters & dimes
his tattoos spilled from his chest
ran down his arms

onto the drivers   the bucket
marked *funeral*
they slid down the hoses
they floated on the Sunday air

they landed on his wife
     the feet of their son
     dashes between dates
     a bouquet of roses

*   *   *

Just two weeks ago
the woman got a promotion

She drove the Dodge two hours
to her son's apartment
in San Bernardino

gave him four twenties
so he could buy schoolbooks
She met his girlfriend   Sonya
& made them
sopapillas & pozole with shrimp

The woman said
I love you
She told the elevator   the parking lot
her '95 Dodge Caravan
the changing lights

the poison sky   the patient traffic
a funeral procession

Transcendence

A good day

MORE ABOUT THE JUNK PILE

When shards of glass
green brown & clear
come up from the ground
littering the cholla & brush
I blame the junk pile

but truth is
whoever lived here ten years ago
an artist
buried her trash

not just glass   four-inch rusted nails
hammers
pull tabs from the '90s
It's all coming back
as I come back
when I throw myself against you

THE GRACKLE

I want to make a list
of things small & bright

The crabapple for instance
the one the pearlescent grackle spared

the larva of the codling moth in the core
that moistens & sucks steadfast

the black seeds

quick deaths

the thumbing of a light switch
the flip of the calendar to

& the rain is—

      oh never mind

I am terrible at lists

& now there is a muscling in of clouds
a noticeable absence   *a missing*
of light to read by

✳   ✳   ✳

About this business of digging down
of tunneling toward
of needling into this rich vein—Come on

any black phoebe knows
a swinging branch is better
when rain comes to the desert

The sun is copper enough
this ammonite fossil from Morocco
golden enough

Me & my man in this cabin

see him outside in his crewneck
covering the wood pile
sopped as bread in a thin stew

not smiling

not smiling until
he sees me looking

*   *   *

& how is it
that we have come in

walking without effort

without exactitude

through the held breath of a Mojave storm
jangling coffee money

       when the firewood is wet as a shipwreck
       & the landlord has called
       to say
       the cabin is being sold?

I guess we are a ball
let go in a stairway
with just enough slope
                    to be called
                        a stairway

We should be drinking whiskey

from miniature bottles stolen
in our linty pockets

The walk to the car
is lengthened
by what we must
return to
as the storm exhales
I look up to see
a hole where something
is expected to return
& nearly step
into a black aurora
of engine oil
but it is
the grackle
at the last
possible
second
&
lifts
to
the
sky

WHISKEY

because it is winter

because we are housesitting for my father

because the whiskey is free

because we had to take care of the dead finch
in the chicken coop

& only one of us could lift the body & know its lightness
before dropping it over the fence
into cholla & brush

because there is so much to keep alive

because I am afraid of my father's dogs

because night ran to cover us & we never asked

whiskey

because my legs stopped working & my body
burned & twitched for a year
        you carried me
        bathed me
        washed my hair

& whiskey

because I'm better now

because some lights are fixed in the sky
& others move in arcs   blinking goodbye
or constant as rivers

WHEN YOU ARE LOST IN THE DESERT
LOOK AT WHAT YOU CAN FIND

The topography
of your shoe treads
the footpaths leading
in & out & in

entire bedroom sets
slashed by hunting knives
& riddled
with bullets

heavy-duty trash bags
each containing
one person's wardrobe
socks & ties & all

cars abandoned with the keys still in the ignition
a bouquet of carnations not yet wilted on the dash
a boxed lunch
still warm on the seat

POEM FOR JOSHUA TREE (9-15-2001)

You say you want to leave
& go back to the city   as if I want you to
stand a little longer in the parking lot
of Sam's Liquor   suffer my home with me

Husked arms stretch
into stars here
in a life sentence of droughts & freezes
& yesterday
a flood rearranged the highway
ruined everybody's yards
drowned a chained-up dog
& still   the tanks from the base in 29 Palms
go west past this lot
hands jaws cocks thumbs
eyes like Pennsylvania sea glass or
Kansas flax or
midnight in Joshua Tree   Pass & pass
hands jaws cocks thumbs

Okay you win   Your arm
I want it heavy on my shoulders
so finish the smokes you bought
& watch the storm-snapped
branches of juniper glowing pink
under Sam's neon sign
the tanks & tanks & tanks

Keep quiet keep watching   keep holding now
the desert's cracked egg
the thick clear single-celled night
all life now everything
running away from us

ACKNOWLEDGMENTS

Poems in this collection first appeared in the following journals, at times in different form:

3 A.M.: "The Worst"
A River and Sound Review: "Hound"
Badlands: "The Burden," "A Dollar (for a funeral)," "Driving East past the Wind Farm on Interstate 10 after a Year of Unemployment"
Bateau: "Shoe Tree"
Borderlands: Texas Poetry Review: "Cops," "Echolalia," "The Road a Silver Ladle"
Breadcrumb Scabs: "New Year's Eve at the Hotel Congress"
Cholla Needles: "Dog & His Man," "Home Invasion (Landers, CA 1992)," "Junk Pile as Seen from inside the Junk Pile," "More about the Junk Pile," "We Were Afraid"
Eclectica: "Story," "We Girls"
Entropy: "The Grackle"
Main Street Rag: "They Danced Me All Afternoon," "Thieving-feet"
RHINO: "Buying Food"
Rust + Moth: "There Is So Much to Say about Lightning"
The Great American Lit Mag: "Winter's Hill or Summer's Lawn"
Tule: "Junk Pile as Seen from My Kitchen Table," "Sometimes Three Hawks Sitting on a Fence Post Means What You Want It to Mean in Victorville, California"

If one can be grateful to a place, grateful in the real way one would be grateful to a steadfast friend, I am then grateful to the desert towns in which I spent my youth. Most of these poems take place in that mysterious, tempestuous, energy-giving landscape. May we do our best to protect the dwindling natural resources in this region.

I would like to thank Perugia Press and Rebecca Olander for choosing *Starshine Road;* Rebecca's warmth, patience, and thoughtful editorial eye served as lamplight through the entire process. My deepest gratitude goes out to all of those writers and teachers who have inspired me to keep at it: Peter Sears, David St. John, Marvin Bell, Kevin Clark, Marsha de la O, Phil Taggart, Molly Bendall, Chad and Jennifer Sweeney, James Cushing, Lisa Coffman, Dian Sousa, Kristin Bock, Leslie St. John, Greg Gilbert, and Paula C. Lowe. Big thanks to Larry Eby for getting my publishing career started. Thank you to Jonathan Maule for staying up late into the night, on many nights, for the sake of poetry, art, and jokes.

My poetry would not be what it is without the influences of my parents—my dad, who taught me desert preparedness and how to lucid dream, and my mother, who showed me how to adapt and flow with grace through the most rugged of environments.

L. I. Henley was born and raised in the Mojave Desert village of Joshua Tree, California. She is the author of two chapbooks, *Desert with a Cabin View* and *The Finding* (both with Orange Monkey Publishing). Her first full-length collection, *These Friends These Rooms,* was published by Big Yes Press in 2016. She is the recipient of The Academy of American Poets University Award, The Duckabush Prize in Poetry, The Orange Monkey Poetry Prize, and The Pangaea Prize through The Poet's Billow. With her husband, poet Jonathan Maule, she lives once again in the high desert of California. Together they edit the online literary and art journal *Aperçus*.

About Perugia Press

Perugia Press publishes one collection of poetry each year, by a woman at the beginning of her publishing career. Our mission is to produce beautiful books that interest long-time readers of poetry and welcome those new to poetry. We also aim to celebrate and promote poetry whenever we can, and to keep the cultural discussion of poetry inclusive.

Also from Perugia Press:

* *Brilliance, Spilling: Twenty Years of Perugia Press Poetry*
* *Guide to the Exhibit,* Lisa Allen Ortiz
* *Grayling,* Jenifer Browne Lawrence
* *Sweet Husk,* Corrie Williamson
* *Begin Empty-Handed,* Gail Martin
* *The Wishing Tomb,* Amanda Auchter
* *Gloss,* Ida Stewart
* *Each Crumbling House,* Melody S. Gee
* *How to Live on Bread and Music,* Jennifer K. Sweeney
* *Two Minutes of Light,* Nancy K. Pearson
* *Beg No Pardon,* Lynne Thompson
* *Lamb,* Frannie Lindsay
* *The Disappearing Letters,* Carol Edelstein
* *Kettle Bottom,* Diane Gilliam Fisher
* *Seamless,* Linda Tomol Pennisi
* *Red,* Melanie Braverman
* *A Wound On Stone,* Faye George
* *The Work of Hands,* Catherine Anderson
* *Reach,* Janet E. Aalfs
* *Impulse to Fly,* Almitra David
* *Finding the Bear,* Gail Thomas

This book is set in Monotype Garamond, a variant of the classic oldstyle serif type family designed in 1922 and 1923. The letterforms are based on the type design work of 17th-century French printer Jean Jannon, whose work was an interpretation of the designs of Claude Garamont, a printer, type designer, and punch cutter who lived and worked in Paris in the 16th century.